Sweet Success

Sweet Success

STEVEN WHEELER

Photographs by Alan Newnham

ANAYA PUBLISHERS LTD.
LONDON

First published in Great Britain in 1990
by Anaya Publishers Ltd, 49 Neal Street, London, WC2H 9PJ.

Managing editor: Janet Illsley
Photographer: Alan Newnham
Designer: Harry Green
Editor: Norma Macmillan
Food stylist: Carole Handslip
Recipe techniques: Mandy Wagstaff
Photographic stylist: Maria Jacques
Calligrapher: Susanne Haines

British Library Cataloguing in Publication Data
Wheeler, Steven
    Sweet success.
    1. Desserts. Recipes
    I. Title
    641.86

    ISBN 1-85470-060-X

Typeset in Great Britain by Tradespools Ltd, Frome, Somerset

Colour reproduction by Columbia Offset, Singapore

Printed and bound in Great Britain
by Clays Ltd, Bungay, Suffolk

CONTENTS

———— ◆ ————

INTRODUCTION

—————————— ◆ ——————————

Illustrated with magnificent colour photographs, *Sweet Success* aims to be both practical and inspirational, and is planned to appeal to beginners and experienced cooks alike. It is divided into nine chapters and ranges from basic meringues to sponges, custards and elaborate pastry confections. Each section begins with a Master Recipe which tells you, step-by-step, how to make a basic preparation. Each Master Recipe is accompanied by a series of what I have called "watchpoints" to help you on your way.

If you are a beginner when it comes to making desserts, you can become totally familiar with a basic technique. You will then acquire the confidence to tackle other more complex recipes and, if you are ever unsure of a technique, you can always refer back to the watchpoint panels alongside every Master Recipe to ensure complete success every time. Those already familiar with all the basic cookery techniques can, of course, skip the step-by-step pages and use the book as a source of ideas for making fabulous international desserts.

Unlike many books on the subject, my aim in writing *Sweet Success* has been to help the reader establish a working knowledge of dessert making and the techniques involved. Experienced cooks will say that cooking is easy, and that while they may follow the occasional recipe, most of the time they make it up as they go along. (This sort of talk is hardly encouraging for those who can barely manage a lump-free custard.) What is it, then, that makes cooking so easy? When I set out to write this book, I asked myself the same question. Admittedly, I did serve a four-year apprenticeship in London and finished up working in Switzerland as a pastry cook, so I might be expected to have a few answers. Cooking is a bit like riding a bicycle: you don't necessarily think about what you are doing, you just get on with it. So, although the answers were in my head, they did take some sorting out. Without realising, for years I had based my understanding of desserts on a simple premise: every recipe I knew was based on one of nine basic preparations; this is how the structure of the book evolved.

My own fascination for desserts began in early childhood as I sat quietly in a corner of the kitchen watching my mother seemingly effortlessly prepare soft, gooey meringues, delicate cakes and custards and perfect ice creams. I made futile efforts to understand the mysteries that lay behind the wonderful aromas as her cakes and pastries emerged from the oven. Children, it seems to me now, were made for desserts and anyone who believes that kids simply demolish them without appreciating the work involved cannot know what it is to be loved and to have parents who spend time in the kitchen preparing food for them. Children are like elephants, they never forget.

This book, then, is written for everyone who like me remembers watching fascinated as their mother cooked, greedily licking spoons when she wasn't looking.

Blackcurrant Granita; Lemon Sorbet; Orange Sorbet.

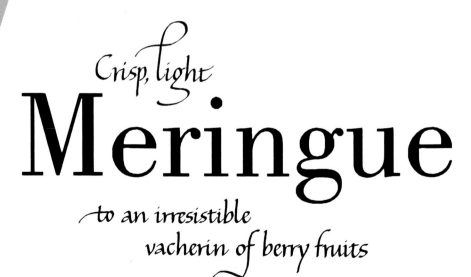

'In cooking, as in all arts, simplicity is the sign of perfection'
CURNONSKY

One of the most useful, and many would say delicious, preparations at the disposal of the pastry cook is the basic meringue. So popular is its use in dessert-making that any dessert that contains meringue in one form or another is bound to be a great success. The most valuable asset of meringue is its ability to retain air, an essential property for soft mousses and smooth creams. When folded into flavoured crème pâtissière, the mixture will rise into an impressive soufflé. Another less common but equally delicious way with meringue is to poach it by floating shapes on hot liquid until set. Alternatively, meringue can be piled in a mould, baked in a *bain marie*, turned out and served with an appropriate sauce. Dried meringue shells or other shapes are always useful in the kitchen, not least for their keeping qualities which make them ideal for creating last-minute desserts. Soft fruits, spirits and liqueurs can be added to meringue to provide additional flavour.

Meringue-making is rarely without its problems. Even with years of experience, I still come across the occasional difficulty. The trick is not to despair but to seek explanation so that you can gain courage to try again. Over time I have encountered various remedies for meringue failures, many of which I have discarded as pure twaddle, but what remains is a collection of useful antidotes. The symptoms that we are all familiar with include reluctant drying, beads of moisture, weepy bottoms, chewy centres, browning and sticking to the paper. I will show you how to deal with these and others in this section.

Crisp, light

Meringue

*to an irresistible
vacherin of berry fruits*

Successful Meringue

Approaching the subject of meringue we are faced with two simple ingredients – egg whites and caster sugar. By adjusting the amounts of sugar to egg white we can vary the density of the meringue according to its use. If we whisk plain egg whites without any sugar at all they will gain volume quickly but will separate easily, thus losing their smoothness. As we add sugar we notice that the meringue gains stability as well as smoothness, making it easy to combine with other ingredients.

The first rule for successful meringue is to ensure perfect cleanliness. The importance of this cannot be overstated since any trace of grease found on or in the equipment and ingredients will prevent the meringue from gaining volume. Mixing bowls are best made of stainless steel, copper or glass and should be cleaned with hot soapy water, rinsed well and dried before use. Soft plastic bowls are prone to harbouring grease so should be avoided. One of the most common faults when making meringue is the contamination of egg whites with egg yolk; traces of stray egg yolk can be removed successfully using a broken egg shell. Open packets of sugar often contain particles of flour or other debris which will in turn prevent the meringue from whisking properly. It is therefore best to open a new packet of sugar when making meringue.

The second rule is to use egg whites at room temperature. If the whites are used straight from the fridge, the cold air in them will contract as they are being whisked, thus preventing the meringue from gaining sufficient volume.

The third rule concerns the method used and the choice of equipment. I choose to whisk egg whites by hand, not for the sake of martyrdom but because I find it a bother to search for, plug in and afterwards clean an electric mixer and its accessories. The hard work associated with hand whisking can be minimized by ensuring that the bowl is held at just below waist level. Resting the bowl on a kitchen stool or in an open drawer should put it at the right height.

Another labour-saving piece of advice concerns the speed at which the egg whites are whisked. There is little profit in whisking at high speed since this has a tendency to knock the air out of the meringue as well as the strength out of your arm very quickly. Hand whisking is a casual affair that relies on efficiency rather than strength. If, after all this soft talk, you prefer to use an electric mixer, note that low speeds will produce a better meringue.

Illustrated overleaf: Blueberry Meringue Tart; Vacherin of Soft Berry Fruits; Oeufs à la Neige.

Oeufs à la Neige

SERVES 4–6

575 ml/1 pint milk

4 eggs, at room temperature

150 g/5 oz caster sugar

½ vanilla pod, or 3 drops of vanilla
    essence

2 tbsp cornflour

2 tbsp cold milk or water

Caramel:

150 g/5 oz caster sugar

Oeufs à la Neige, Snow Eggs or Floating Islands as they are often called, are lightly poached meringue ovals floating on a vanilla-scented custard and topped with a rich, dark caramel. This is a classical dessert that features in many of the finest restaurants. It is designed for guests who have over-indulged on their main course and require a sweet little nothing to smooth the palate before coffee.

───── ◆ ─────

Pour the milk into a large shallow saucepan and bring to a simmer. Separate the egg whites into a clean mixing bowl; put the yolks in another bowl. Whisk the egg whites until they will hold their own weight on the whisk. Add 75 g/3 oz of the sugar a little at a time, and continue whisking until stiff peaks form.

Shape the meringue into ovals between two tablespoons dipped in warm water, and float the shapes on the simmering milk. Poach gently for 2 minutes, turning once; do not allow the milk to boil rapidly or the meringues will tend to soufflé and lose their shape. Carefully lift the meringues, which will be soft but firm to touch, out of the milk and place on a tray lined with a damp tea towel.

To prepare the vanilla custard, split the vanilla pod open to reveal the tiny black seeds and add to the hot poaching milk, or add the vanilla essence. Add the remaining caster sugar and the cornflour to the egg yolks with the cold milk or water and stir until smooth. Pour the poaching milk over the egg yolk mixture and stir to mix, then pour into a smaller heavy saucepan. Stir the custard to the boil and simmer briefly to thicken. Strain the custard into a serving bowl and allow to cool to room temperature, then float the meringues on top.

To prepare the caramel, measure 2 tbsp of the sugar into a small heavy saucepan and melt over a moderate heat until liquid but not brown. Add a further 2 tbsp of the sugar and stir until dissolved. Continue to add the sugar in this way, then allow to caramelize to a deep mahogany brown. Without delay, spoon the caramel over the white meringues.

Oeufs à la Neige can be made up to 3 hours before serving, and are best eaten the same day.

Illustrated on page 11

Vacherin of Soft Berry Fruits

SERVES 6–8

5 egg whites, at room temperature

225 g/8 oz caster sugar

150 g/5 oz icing sugar

Filling:

425 ml/15 fl oz double cream

3 tbsp caster sugar

2 tbsp dry sherry, Kirsch or Grand
　Marnier

350 g/12 oz fresh or frozen mixed
　raspberries, blackberries,
　redcurrants and strawberries

To finish:

cluster of fresh redcurrants and
　blackcurrants, or 15 g/½ oz
　crystallized violets or rose petals

The vacherin is known amongst French pastry buffs as the European version of the Australian Pavlova. The difference is that the Pavlova has a deep, soft meringue base, whereas the vacherin has a crisp case. Both are filled with a mixture of fresh fruit and cream. The vacherin has the advantage that it can be made well in advance and stored in an airtight container ready for use.

♦

Preheat the oven to 140°C/275°F/gas 1. Line two wooden baking trays with non-stick baking parchment (see page 12). Draw a 23 cm/9 inch circle on one of the baking trays, using a plate of the same size as a guide. Set aside.

Whisk 4 of the egg whites in a clean mixing bowl until they will hold their weight on the whisk. Add the caster sugar a little at a time, continuing to whisk until stiff and shiny. Spoon the meringue into a large piping bag fitted with a large plain nozzle.

Pipe the meringue in a continuous spiral within the marked circle, starting in the centre. Pipe the remainder of the meringue into twenty 6 cm/2½ inch oval shells on the other baking tray. Dry the meringues in the preheated oven for 15 minutes, then reduce the temperature of the oven to 120°C/250°F/gas ½ and leave the meringues to dry in the oven for a further 2–3 hours. Allow to cool completely.

To assemble the vacherin case, put the remaining egg white into a mixing bowl and stir in the icing sugar. Use to secure 12 meringue shells around the edge of the meringue base, overlapping them slightly.

To prepare the filling, loosely whip the cream with the caster sugar and flavour with sherry, Kirsch or Grand Marnier, according to taste. Break up the remaining meringue shells and fold into the cream. Turn into the centre of the meringue case. Scatter the soft fruits over the cream and decorate with clusters of fresh currants, crystallized violets or rose petals, as desired. Serve within 1 hour of assembling.

Illustrated on page 10

VARIATION

Tropical Fruit Vacherin: Fold 25 g/1 oz desiccated coconut into the meringue mixture. Dip the meringue shells in melted chocolate and assemble the case. Flavour filling with rum and top with tropical fruits – mango, kiwi fruit, pineapple, banana, paw paw or papaya, and passion fruit.

Meringue Bombe Jewelled with Ruby Fruits

WATCHPOINTS
◆
Meringue ◆ Egg Custard

SERVES 4

soft butter for greasing

50 g/2 oz flaked almonds, toasted

4 egg whites, at room temperature

125 g/4 oz caster sugar

225 g/8 oz mixed berry fruits, fresh
or frozen, such as strawberries,
raspberries, redcurrants,
blackcurrants, blackberries

¾ recipe Egg Custard Sauce (page
39), cooled

Preheat the oven to 180°C/350°F/gas 4. Lightly grease an 18 cm/7 inch soufflé dish or a 1.1 litre/2 pint bombe mould with the soft butter, cover base and sides with toasted almonds and put to one side.

Separate the egg whites into a clean mixing bowl and whisk until they will hold their weight on the whisk, then add the sugar a little at a time and continue whisking until stiff. Fold in the chosen fruit, and turn into the prepared mould.

Stand the mould in a roasting pan, half fill the pan with boiling water and bake in the preheated oven for 25 minutes. Allow the bombe to cool a little before turning out on to a serving dish. Serve with the custard.

Fresh Fruit Pavlova

WATCHPOINTS
◆
Meringue

SERVES 6–8

4 egg whites, at room temperature

225 g/8 oz caster sugar

1 tsp white wine vinegar

1 tsp cornflour

Filling:

275 ml/10 fl oz double cream

2 tbsp caster sugar

2 tbsp eau-de-vie de Framboise,
Kirsch or dry sherry

450 g/1 lb raspberries, fresh or
frozen, or other berry fruits

50 g/2 oz flaked almonds, toasted

icing sugar for sprinkling

Brittle on the outside, internally soft, Pavlovas belong to the season of soft berry fruits which can be seen at their best nestling in cream and meringue.

———— ◆ ————

Preheat the oven to 140°/275°F/gas 1. Line a wooden baking tray with non-stick baking parchment and mark on it a 20 cm/8 inch circle. (see page 12). Set aside.

Place the egg whites in a clean mixing bowl and whisk until they will hold their weight on the whisk. Add the sugar a little at a time, continuing to whisk until stiff and shiny. Add the wine vinegar and cornflour and stir briefly.

Spread the meringue on the drawn circle to cover. Transfer to the preheated oven and bake for 2 hours. Allow to cool completely.

To prepare the filling, loosely whip the cream with the sugar and flavour with the liqueur or sherry.

To assemble the Pavlova, spread half of the cream over the meringue base and pile on half of the raspberries. Cover with the remaining cream and raspberries followed by a sprinkling of toasted flaked almonds and icing sugar. Once assembled, Pavlovas are best eaten within 3–4 hours.

*Meringue Bombe Jewelled
with Ruby Fruits;
Fresh Fruit Pavlova.*

Crème Brûlée aux Fruits des Bois

My favourite crème brûlée is as smooth and as near liquid yellow as an over-ripe Normandy cheese and contains a wave of soft berry fruits. The best caramel tops are crisp and dark with a slight bitter taste.

———————— ◆ ————————

SERVES 4

175 g/6 oz raspberries, blueberries or alpine strawberries
6 egg yolks
2 tbsp caster sugar
275 ml/10 fl oz double cream
1/2 vanilla pod, split
125 g/4 oz demerara sugar

To decorate:
berry fruits

Divide the fruit between four 9 cm/3 1/2 inch diameter ramekins.

Place the egg yolks in a bowl and stir in the sugar with a hand whisk. Put the cream and vanilla pod in a heavy saucepan and bring to the boil. Pour over the egg yolks and stir until evenly mixed.

Pour the custard back into the saucepan and stir over a low heat until it will just coat the back of the spoon, 20–30 seconds. Without delay, strain into the flameproof dishes and chill to set.

Sprinkle the demerara sugar evenly over the custards and place under a hot grill to caramelize. Chill before serving, decorated with berry fruits.

Petits Pots de Crème au Chocolat; Crème Brûlée aux Fruits des Bois.

Petits Pots de Crème au Chocolat

MAKES 8

575 ml/1 pint milk
4 egg yolks
1 egg
50 g/2 oz caster sugar
3 tbsp cold water
125 g/4 oz best quality plain chocolate, broken into pieces

To decorate:
whipped cream
chopped nuts
chocolate leaves (optional)

Preheat the oven to 180°C/350°F/gas 4. Arrange eight custard pots or ramekin dishes in a roasting pan and set side.

Bring the milk to the boil in a heavy saucepan. Mix three of the egg yolks, the whole egg and 25 g/1 oz of the sugar in a bowl. Pour over the boiling milk, stirring evenly.

Dissolve the remaining sugar in the water over low heat. Remove from the heat and stir in the chocolate until melted, followed by the remaining egg yolk. Stir a little of the custard into the chocolate mixture, then combine with the remainder.

Strain the custard into a jug and pour into the custard pots or ramekins. Half fill the roasting pan with boiling water and place in the preheated oven for 25–30 minutes or until the custards seem firm when the sides of the pots are tapped. Allow to cool and chill before serving. Decorate with piped cream rosettes, chopped nuts and chocolate leaves if desired.

Strawberry Yogurt Ice

SERVES 6–8

275 g/10 oz strawberries,
  fresh or frozen
50 g/2 oz icing sugar, sifted
275 ml/10 fl oz plain yogurt
finely grated zest and juice
  of ½ orange

Hull the strawberries and cut them in half. Purée the berries together with the icing sugar in a food processor or blender. Add the yogurt and orange zest and juice and blend until smooth.

For best results, freeze the mixture in an electric ice cream maker, allowing about 25 minutes until firm. If you do not have an ice cream maker, transfer the mixture to a stainless steel or enamel bowl and freeze for 1 hour or until the mixture begins to freeze around the edges.

Whisk well to break down the ice crystals evenly. Return to the freezer and freeze for a further 1–1½ hours, whisking every 20 minutes, until firm.

Transfer the yogurt ice to a plastic container, cover and store in the ice compartment of your refrigerator.

VARIATION

Raspberry Yogurt Ice: Replace strawberries with raspberries. Omit the orange. After puréeing the raspberries with the icing sugar, sieve to remove pips. Freeze as above.

Blackcurrant Yogurt Ice

SERVES 4–6

175 g/6 oz blackcurrants, fresh,
  frozen or canned
75 ml/3 fl oz water
75 g/3 oz granulated sugar
275 ml/10 fl oz plain yogurt

If using fresh or frozen blackcurrants, place them in a stainless steel saucepan with the water and sugar, cover and simmer for 6–8 minutes. Rub the soft berries through a nylon sieve together with their juices. If using canned blackcurrants, just sieve them with their syrup. Combine the blackcurrant purée with the yogurt.

For best results, freeze in an electric ice cream maker. If you do not have an ice cream maker, transfer the mixture to a stainless steel or enamel bowl and freeze for 1 hour or until the mixture begins to freeze around the edges. Whisk well to break down the ice crystals evenly. Return to the freezer and freeze for a further 1-1½ hours, whisking every 20 minutes, until firm.

Transfer the yogurt ice to a plastic container, cover and store in the ice compartment of your refrigerator until ready to use.

*Strawberry Yogurt Ice;
Blackcurrant Yogurt Ice.*

Lemon Sorbet

WATCHPOINTS
◆
Ice Cream & Sorbet

SERVES 4–6
575 ml/1 pint water
225 g/8 oz granulated sugar
275 ml/10 fl oz fresh lemon juice
(5–6 large lemons)

Orange Sorbet in ice bowl;
Lemon Sorbet;
Lime Sorbet;
Pineapple Sorbet Wedges.

Measure the water and sugar into a saucepan and bring to a simmer, stirring until dissolved. Allow the syrup to cool completely, then stir in the lemon juice and strain.

Transfer the mixture to a stainless steel or enamel bowl and freeze for 1 hour or until the mixture is just beginning to set at the edges. Whisk well to break down the ice crystals evenly. Return to the freezer and freeze for a further 1½–2 hours, whisking every 30 minutes, until firm.

Transfer the sorbet to a plastic container, cover and store in the ice compartment of your refrigerator until required.

VARIATIONS:
Orange Sorbet: Replace the lemon juice with freshly squeezed orange Juice.
Lime Sorbet: Replace the lemon juice with freshly squeezed lime juice and 1–2 drops green food colouring.

Pineapple Sorbet Wedges

WATCHPOINTS
◆
Ice Cream & Sorbet

SERVES 6
150 ml/5 fl oz water
75 g/3 oz granulated sugar
1 large pineapple
2 tbsp Kirsch

Measure the water and sugar into a saucepan, bring to the boil, stirring to dissolve the sugar, and simmer for 2–3 minutes. Pour the syrup into a metal bowl and cool over ice. In the meantime, cut the pineapple in half lengthwise, discard core and spoon out flesh. Set the pineapple skins aside. Place the flesh in a blender or food processor and work until smooth. Transfer to a measuring jug and top up if necessary with water to make 250 ml/9 fl oz.

Stir the pineapple juice and Kirsch into the cool syrup and freeze for 30 minutes or until the mixture is beginning to set at the edges.

Remove sorbet from freezer and whisk to break up any pieces of ice. Return to the freezer and freeze for a further 1½ hours, whisking every 30 minutes, until slushy. Pile the sorbet into the pineapple shells, spread level and freeze for 1 hour or until firm.

To serve, cut each pineapple half into 3 wedges and keep in the ice compartment of the refrigerator until needed.

Frankfurter Kranz

WATCHPOINTS

♦

Caramel ♦ Classic Sponge Cake ♦ Crème Pâtissière

SERVES 6–8

Sponge:

175 g/6 oz soft unsalted butter, plus
   a little extra for greasing
175 g/6 oz caster sugar
3 eggs, at room temperature, beaten
175 g/6 oz self-raising flour

Syrup:

3 tbsp golden syrup
150 ml/5 fl oz boiling water
2 tbsp Kirsch or Grand Marnier

To finish:

1 recipe crème diplomat (page 27)
1 recipe almond praline (page 69),
   crushed
8 candied mimosa
candied angelica strips

*Frankfurter Kranz;
Caramelized Apple
Sponge Cake.*

No, it's not a hotdog nor does it belong in a bun. Frankfurter Kranz is a delicious sponge baked in an angel cake tin, moistened with a Kirsch syrup, layered with crème diplomat and masked with crushed praline.

♦

Preheat the oven to 180°C/350°F/gas 4. Grease a 20 cm/8 inch angel cake tin and dust with flour.

To make the sponge, beat the butter and sugar together until pale and fluffy. Add eggs a little at a time and beat until smooth. Fold in the flour.

Turn into the prepared tin and bake in the centre of the preheated oven for 40–45 minutes or until a skewer inserted into the centre comes away cleanly. Turn out on to a wire rack to cool.

Slice the cake into three layers. Combine the syrup ingredients together and use to moisten each cake layer. Sandwich the layers together with crème diplomat. Cover the cake with the remaining crème diplomat and press on the crushed praline. Decorate with candied mimosa and angelica.

SERVES 6

soft butter for greasing
75 g/3 oz butter
900 g/2 lb dessert apples, peeled,
   quartered and cored
4 tbsp caster sugar
2 tbsp water

Sponge:

3 eggs, size 2–3, at room
   temperature
75 g/3 oz caster sugar
75 g/3 oz plain flour

Caramelized Apple Sponge Cake

WATCHPOINTS

♦

Caramel ♦ Whisked Sponge

Lightly grease a 20 cm/8 inch cake tin. Line the base with greaseproof paper and dust the sides with flour. Preheat the oven to 190°C/375°F/gas 5.

Melt half of the butter in a large frying pan, add the apples and toss in the butter for 6–8 minutes until golden. Spoon into the bottom of the cake tin.

Dissolve sugar in water in frying pan, then simmer until it begins to caramelize, 4–5 minutes. Stir in remaining butter and pour over apples.

To prepare the sponge, whisk the eggs and sugar together in a mixing bowl until the mixture is thick enough to leave a lasting ribbon across the surface, 3–4 minutes. Sift the flour over and fold in with a metal spoon.

Pour the sponge mixture over the apples. Bake in the centre of the preheated oven for 30–35 minutes. To serve, run a knife around the edge of the cake, invert on to a serving dish and serve hot, with custard sauce.

Poires Belle Hélène

WATCHPOINTS
– ◆ –
Fruit

SERVES 4
850 ml/1½ pints water
175 g/6 oz granulated sugar
juice of ½ lemon, or two 50 mg
     vitamin C tablets
1 vanilla pod, or 1 tsp vanilla essence
4 dessert pears

Hot chocolate sauce:
150 ml/5 fl oz single cream or milk
1 tbsp caster sugar
175 g/6 oz best quality plain
     chocolate, chopped

To finish:
1 litre/1¾ pints vanilla ice cream
     (page 53)
50 g/2 oz flaked almonds, toasted

For this stunningly simple dessert we owe our gratitude to the master chef Georges Auguste Escoffier who created it originally as a lady's dessert. Poires Belle Hélène consists of a poached pear served with vanilla ice cream and hot chocolate sauce to create a delicious contrast.

———— ◆ ————

Measure the water and sugar into a saucepan, add the lemon juice or vitamin C tablets and vanilla and bring to the boil. Leave to simmer while you peel the pears. Peel the pears from top to bottom with a vegetable peeler and scoop out the inside cores with a melon scoop, working from the bases. Place the pears in the syrup, cover with a circle of greaseproof paper and simmer for 20–25 minutes or until tender. Allow to cool, then chill.

To make the chocolate sauce put the cream or milk and sugar into a heavy saucepan and bring to the boil. Remove from the heat, add the chocolate and stir until melted.

To serve, scoop the vanilla ice cream into individual dishes and stand a pear in each. Pour the hot chocolate sauce over and sprinkle with almonds.

Clafoutis

SERVES 4
2 tbsp plain flour
2 tbsp caster sugar
1 good pinch ground cinnamon
225 ml/8 fl oz milk
2 eggs
1 tbsp Kirsch or Cognac (optional)
450 g/1 lb fresh tart black cherries,
     or 450 g/1 lb bottled black
     cherries
soft butter for greasing
icing sugar for dusting

This simple French dessert is made by baking a layer of dark cherries in a pancake batter until crisp and golden.

———— ◆ ————

To prepare the batter, place the flour, sugar and cinnamon in a bowl. Add one third of the milk and stir to a smooth paste. Add the remaining milk with the eggs and, if using, the Kirsch or Cognac. Allow to stand for 30–40 minutes before using.

Preheat the oven to 190°C/375°F/gas 5. Stone the cherries and arrange in a single layer in a lightly greased gratin dish. Pour the batter over to three-quarters cover the cherries. Bake in the preheated oven for 40–45 minutes. Dust with sifted icing sugar, and serve warm or cold, with cream.

Poires Belle Hélène; Clafoutis.

Pêches Rafraîchis Bourguignonne

WATCHPOINTS
– ◆ –
Fruit

SERVES 4

450 g/1 lb raspberries, fresh or frozen

175 ml/6 fl oz Beaujolais or other fruity red wine

3 tbsp icing sugar

8 ripe peaches

To decorate:

raspberries or raspberry leaves

50 g/2 oz flaked almonds, toasted (optional)

Bring me some beautifully ripe peaches, some sweet-scented raspberries and a bottle of Beaujolais wine and I will show you how to prepare one of the most talked-about desserts this side of the crème brûlée.

───────── ◆ ─────────

Purée the raspberries in a blender then rub through a nylon sieve into a bowl. Stir in the wine and icing sugar.

Place the peaches in a large bowl, cover with boiling water and leave for 20–30 seconds. Drain the peaches, plunge into cold water, then peel. Slice into the sauce and leave to macerate for 1¹/₂-2 hours, or longer. Serve decorated with raspberries or leaves, and flaked almonds if desired.

Frozen Pineapple and Orange Soufflé; Pêches Refraîchis Bourguignonne.

Frozen Pineapple and Orange Soufflé

WATCHPOINTS
◆
Whisked Sponge ◆ Fruit

SERVES 8

4 oranges

4 small macaroons or sponge fingers (page 101), coarsely crumbled

2 tbsp dark rum

3 eggs, at room temperature

150 g/5 oz caster sugar

2 tsp powdered gelatine

1 tbsp cold water

275 ml/10 fl oz double cream, softly whipped

75 g/3 oz pineapple, cored and crushed or finely chopped

Cut a piece of stiff paper to fit around the edge of a 15 cm/6 inch soufflé dish so as to raise the edge by 5 cm/2 inches and secure with freezer tape.

Scrub two of the oranges with warm soapy water and rinse well to remove their waxy veneer, then grate the zest finely. Peel and segment these oranges; reserve for decoration. Remove the peel and pith from the other two oranges and roughly chop the flesh.

Soak the macaroons or sponge fingers in the rum.

Whisk the eggs and sugar together until thick enough to leave a lasting ribbon across the surface. Soften the gelatine in the cold water, then dissolve over a pan of boiling water. Add to the egg mixture and whisk in the grated orange zest. Fold in the cream, then gently stir in the chopped orange and pineapple together with the rum-soaked macaroons.

Pile the mixture into the prepared soufflé dish and freeze for 2¹/₂-3 hours. Test with a knife to ensure the soufflé is soft enough to serve.

To serve, remove the paper collar from the dish and decorate the soufflé with orange segments.

Blueberry Cheesecake

SERVES 8

75 g/3 oz unsalted butter
175 g/6 oz semi-sweet biscuits
1 tbsp powdered gelatine
2 tbsp cold water
350 g/12 oz full fat soft cheese
275 ml/10 fl oz plain yogurt
75 g/3 oz caster sugar
3 egg whites, at room temperature
150 ml/5 fl oz whipping cream,
   whipped until thick
350 g/12 oz blueberries

Glaze:
175 ml/6 fl oz water
2 tbsp caster sugar
1 tbsp arrowroot

Cheesecakes are a popular finish to any meal and are especially attractive when decorated with seasonal fruits. This basic recipe may be adapted to use any number of summer fruits as a delicious topping.

——————— ♦ ———————

Grease a 20 cm/8 inch loose-bottomed cake tin. Line the bottom with a round of greaseproof paper and the sides with a narrow strip.

Melt the butter in a small saucepan. Finely crush the biscuits in a polythene bag, using a rolling pin, and stir into the melted butter. Spread the crumbs over the bottom of the cake tin and press down into an even layer with the back of a spoon. Set aside.

Sprinkle the gelatine into a small cup or bowl containing the cold water. Leave to soften for a few minutes, then stand the bowl in a saucepan of simmering water and stir until the gelatine has completely dissolved.

Place the soft cheese, yogurt and 25 g/1 oz of the sugar in a mixing bowl and blend together until even. Whisk the egg whites in a large clean bowl until they will hold their weight on the whisk. Add the remaining sugar a little at a time, whisking until the whites will hold a stiff peak. Stir the gelatine into the cheese mixture, then add the whipped cream and whisked egg whites and fold together with a large metal spoon or spatula. Fold in half of the blueberries.

Turn into the prepared cake tin and cover. Refrigerate for at least 2 hours or until set.

To make the glaze, put 1 tbsp of the water in a small cup and the remainder in a saucepan. Add the sugar to the pan and bring to the boil, stirring to dissolve the sugar. Boil to make a light syrup. Mix the arrowroot with the water in the cup, then stir into the boiling syrup and simmer until thickened. Allow to cool slightly.

Add the remaining blueberries to the glaze, and spoon the mixture over the top of the cheesecake. Allow the glaze to cool completely and set before removing the cheesecake from the tin.

Blueberry Cheesecake; Strawberries Romanoff (page 92).

Gooseberry Tea Cake

WATCHPOINTS
◆
Classic Sponge Cake

SERVES 9–12

125 g/4 oz soft butter, plus a little extra for greasing

125 g/4 oz caster sugar

2 eggs, at room temperature, beaten

75 g/3 oz self-raising flour

3 tbsp ground almonds

1 pinch ground mace

finely grated zest of ½ orange

125 g/4 oz gooseberries, topped and tailed

Topping (optional):

50 g/2 oz blanched almonds, chopped

If fresh gooseberries are not available use bottled ones, or try fresh apricots, redcurrants or cherries.

———————— ◆ ————————

Preheat the oven to 180°C/350°F/gas 4. Lightly grease a 1 kg/2 lb loaf tin with soft butter and line with greaseproof paper.

Place the soft butter and sugar in a mixing bowl and beat together until pale and fluffy. Gradually add the eggs and beat until smooth. Sift the flour, ground almonds and mace together into the bowl, add the finely grated orange zest and stir together. Fold in the gooseberries.

Turn into the prepared loaf tin and sprinkle with almonds if desired. Bake in the centre of the preheated oven for 50–55 minutes or until well risen and golden and a skewer inserted into the middle will come away cleanly. Allow to cool in the tin.

Rich Fig and Walnut Tea Cake; Gooseberry Tea Cake.

SERVES 9–12

150 g/5 oz soft butter, plus a little extra for greasing

125 g/4 oz dried figs, roughly chopped

1 tea bag

200 ml/7 fl oz boiling water

½ tsp orange-flower water (optional)

150 g/5 oz soft brown sugar

2 eggs, at room temperature, beaten

150 g/5 oz self-raising flour, sifted

50 g/2 oz shelled walnuts, ground

finely grated zest of 1 orange

Rich Fig and Walnut Tea Cake

WATCHPOINTS
◆
Classic Sponge Cake

For this recipe I have moistened dried figs in tea flavoured with a hint of orange before mixing them into a basic sponge enriched with ground walnuts. The cake is deliciously moist and improves with keeping for 1–2 days.

———————— ◆ ————————

Preheat the oven to 180°C/350°F/gas 4. Lightly grease an 18 cm/7 inch round cake tin with soft butter and line with greaseproof paper.

Place the figs and the tea bag in a bowl, pour over the boiling water and add the orange-flower water, if using. Leave to stand for 10–15 minutes.

Beat the soft butter and sugar together in another bowl until pale and fluffy. Add the eggs a little at a time and beat until smooth. Stir in the flour, ground walnuts and orange zest. Drain the figs and fold into the mixture.

Turn the mixture into the prepared cake tin and bake in the preheated oven for 1–1¼ hours or until a skewer inserted into the centre will come away cleanly. Allow to cool in the tin.

Carrot and Hazelnut Spice Cake

SERVES 8–10

150 g/5 oz soft butter, plus a little
    extra for greasing

150 g/5 oz caster sugar

2 eggs, at room temperature, beaten

150 g/5 oz self-raising flour, sifted

$\frac{1}{2}$ tsp ground cinnamon

50 g/2 oz shelled hazelnuts, ground

175 g/6 oz carrots, peeled and
    coarsely grated

*Carrot and Hazelnut
Spice Cake;
Sticky Banana Cake
with Dark Chocolate
Chips.*

Whoever discovered that carrots could be baked into a deliciously moist cake must have been met with a certain amount of scepticism from those who for centuries had been eating carrots in savoury stews and soups!

———— ♦ ————

Preheat the oven to 180°C/350°F/gas 4. Lightly grease an 18 cm/7 inch round cake tin with soft butter and line with greaseproof paper.

Beat the soft butter and sugar together in a bowl until pale and fluffy. Gradually add the eggs and beat until smooth. (If the mixture begins to separate, stir in a little of the flour.) Combine the flour, cinnamon, hazelnuts and carrot, then fold into the mixture.

Turn into the prepared cake tin and bake in the centre of the preheated oven for 1 hour or until a skewer inserted into the centre comes away cleanly. Allow to cool in the tin.

Sticky Banana Cake with Dark Chocolate Chips

SERVES 8–10

125 g/4 oz soft butter, plus a little
    extra for greasing

150 g/5 oz soft brown sugar

2 eggs, at room temperature, beaten

3 medium-size ripe bananas, mashed

250 g/9 oz self-raising flour

1 pinch ground allspice

1 pinch salt

75 g/3 oz dark chocolate chips

There is only one thing better than a sticky banana cake and that is a sticky banana cake riddled with chocolate chips.

———— ♦ ————

Preheat the oven to 180°C/350°F/gas 4. Lightly grease a 1 kg/2 lb loaf tin or 18 cm/7 inch round cake tin with butter and line with greaseproof paper.

Beat the soft butter and sugar together in a bowl until pale and fluffy. Add the eggs a little at a time and beat until smooth. Add the mashed bananas. Sift the flour, allspice and salt together over the mixture, add the chocolate chips and fold in.

Turn the mixture into the prepared cake tin and bake in the centre of the preheated oven for 50 minutes to 1 hour or until a skewer inserted into the centre comes away cleanly. Allow to cool in the tin.

Store in an airtight container. The texture and flavour of this cake will improve if kept for a day or so before serving.

Black Forest Gâteau

WATCHPOINTS
◆
Whisked Sponge

SERVES 8

one 20 cm/8 inch rich chocolate
whisked sponge (page 119)
75 g/3 oz caster sugar
200 ml/7 fl oz boiling water
2 tbsp Kirsch

Filling:

350 g/12 oz jar stoned black cherries
in syrup
2 tbsp arrowroot
3 tbsp cold water
275 ml/10 fl oz double cream

To decorate:

200 g/7 oz best quality plain
chocolate, grated
8 fresh cherries

This irresistible dark, moist chocolate gâteau is riddled with black cherries, Kirsch and whipped cream.

———— ◆ ————

To prepare the filling, drain the cherries, reserving 200 ml/7 fl oz of the syrup. Mix the arrowroot with the cold water. Bring the syrup to the boil in a saucepan, stir in the arrowroot and simmer to thicken. Stir in the cherries and allow to cool. Softly whip the cream.

Slice the sponge into three layers. Dissolve the caster sugar in the boiling water to make a syrup. Moisten the sponge layers with the syrup, then sprinkle with the Kirsch.

To assemble the gâteau, spread a layer of cream over the first sponge layer and top with half of the cherries. Sandwich the second layer in the same way. Position the final layer on top and cover the top and side of the cake with a thin layer of cream. Mask the entire cake with grated chocolate. Pipe eight blobs of cream around the top of the gâteau and decorate with cherries.

*Black Forest Gâteau;
Dark Chocolate and
Chestnut Roulade.*

Dark Chocolate and Chestnut Roulade

WATCHPOINTS
◆
Whisked Sponge

SERVES 6–8

1 chocolate Swiss roll sponge
(page 119)

Filling:

275 ml/10 fl oz whipping cream
1/2 tsp vanilla essence
125 g/4 oz canned sweetened
chestnut purée

To decorate:

150 ml/5 fl oz whipping cream
6–8 pieces candied chestnut
(*marrons glacés*)
caster sugar for dusting
6–8 strips candied angelica

As an alternative to this roulade's delicious chestnut filling, try crème pâtissière flavoured with praline, crème diplomat or whipped cream flavoured with vanilla.

———— ◆ ————

To make the filling, softly whip the cream with the vanilla essence. Stir a little of the whipped cream into the chestnut purée, then carefully fold in the remainder.

Place the chocolate sponge face down on a clean sheet of greaseproof paper and spread the chestnut filling over the sponge. Roll up from a short end, lifting the sponge carefully with the help of the paper.

To decorate, spoon or pipe blobs of cream along the top of the roulade. Top with candied chestnut pieces rolled in caster sugar and angelica.

Sherry Trifle

WATCHPOINTS
◆
Whisked Sponge ◆ Egg Custard

SERVES 8

one 20 cm/8 inch plain whisked
    sponge (page 119)
4 tbsp red jam
225 g/8 oz raspberries or redcurrants
    (fresh or frozen)

Syrup:
4 tbsp golden syrup
150 ml/5 fl oz boiling water
5 tbsp medium sherry

Custard:
575 ml/1 pint milk
3 drops vanilla essence
3 tbsp custard powder
3 egg yolks
2 tbsp caster sugar

Topping:
150 ml/5 fl oz double cream
50 g/2 oz flaked almonds, toasted

Slice the sponge into three layers and sandwich back together with jam. Cut into large cubes and scatter into the bottom of a trifle bowl, together with the raspberries and redcurrants, reserving a few for decoration.

To make the syrup, dissolve the golden syrup in the boiling water and pour over the sponge to moisten. Sprinkle on the sherry and set aside.

To make the custard, measure 3 tbsp of the milk into a bowl. Put the remainder in a heavy saucepan, add the vanilla essence and bring to the boil. Add the custard powder, egg yolks and sugar to the bowl and stir until smoothly blended. When the milk has come to the boil, stir into the custard mixture, then return to the saucepan and simmer gently to thicken, stirring constantly. Pour the custard over the sponge and leave to cool completely.

To finish, softly whip the cream and spread a thin layer over the surface of the trifle. Pipe on a decorative border. Sprinkle with toasted almonds and decorate with reserved fruit. Chill before serving.

Sherry Trifle;
Viennese Pancakes with
Soft Fruit Centres.

SERVES 6

1 recipe Swiss roll mixture
    (page 119)
450 g/1 lb mixed soft fruits such as
    strawberries, raspberries,
    redcurrants, blackcurrants,
    peaches or tropical fruits
1 recipe crème diplomat (page 27) or
    275 ml/10 fl oz double cream,
    whipped
icing sugar for dusting

Viennese Pancakes with Soft Fruit Centres

WATCHPOINTS
◆
Whisked Sponge ◆ Crème Pâtissière

These delicious sponge pancakes are folded over a mixture of soft berry fruits and cream, dusted with icing sugar and served as a dessert or pâtisserie.

———————— ◆ ————————

Preheat the oven to 220°C/425°F/gas 7. Line two 38 × 30 cm/15 × 12 inch baking sheets with greaseproof paper.

Spoon the sponge mixture into three heaps on each baking sheet and spread into six rounds, roughly 15 cm/6 inches in diameter. Bake in the preheated oven for 8–10 minutes or until springy to the touch.

Spread out a clean tea towel on the work surface. Turn the sponge rounds upside down on to the tea towel. Leave to cool.

Fold the fruits into the crème diplomat or cream. Divide between the sponge pancakes, fold over in half and dust with sifted icing sugar.

1

Never attempt pastry if you are short of time or in a bad mood.

2

Pastry is best made early in the morning when it is cool.

3

The finest pastry is made by hand.

4

Weigh all ingredients, and make sure you understand the recipe before commencing.

5

During warm weather, butter and margarine should be used straight from the refrigerator.

6

In any pastry recipe, you can substitute wholemeal flour for half of the white flour. In this case, you may have to use more liquid.

RUBBING IN

7

Soft spreading margarines are not suitable for rubbing in. Choose block margarine or butter. Unsalted butter has a cleaner fresher flavour than many salted butters.

8

To avoid aching shoulders whilst rubbing in, position the bowl at just below waist level. If necessary stand the mixing bowl on a tea towel, on a kitchen stool.

9

Aim to incorporate as much air as possible, and to achieve an even distribution of fat through the flour.

10

Do not allow the fat to soften and become absorbed. Flour that has absorbed melted fat will not absorb water and form into a coherent dough. Such a dough is inclined to crumble and fall apart.

11

If for some reason the fat does begin to melt and feel oily, place in the refrigerator to chill and firm for 20–30 minutes.

12

Work speedily, especially in warm weather and if you are inclined to have warm hands.

13

If you are distracted whilst making pastry and have to leave the kitchen, place the mixing bowl in the refrigerator.

ADDING THE LIQUID

14

Liquids must be as cool as possible to retain the essential coolness of the pastry.

15

Liquids must be added all at once, never in dribs and drabs. It is better to add extra flour to a pastry that is too wet than to add extra water to one that is too dry.

16

Never knead a pastry. If using an electric mixer or food processor, avoid over-mixing.

RESTING

17

Pastries which have water added must be allowed to rest for at least 45 minutes before use. Pastry that is not allowed sufficient resting time is liable to toughen when baked.

18

When freezing uncooked pastry, remember to first allow resting time because pastry cannot rest during freezing.

Shortcrust Pastry

Shortcrust pastry is the most basic type of pastry and can be used for sweet as well as savoury pies, flans, tarts and turnovers. The basic recipe can be easily remembered as half fat to flour, with the amount of water half that of the fat.

MAKES 350 g/12 oz
225 g/8 oz plain flour
1 large pinch salt
100 g/4 oz cool butter or margarine
3–4 tbsp cold water

bowl, running thumbs from little finger to index finger, breaking through any large lumps of fat. Lightness is incorporated by lifting the mixture out of the bowl and allowing it to fall through the air. Continue rubbing in until the mixture resembles fine fresh breadcrumbs and tiny pieces of fat are still visible.

Over-mixing should be avoided where possible. Turn the dough onto a floured surface and knead lightly. Cover the pastry with cling film and allow to rest in the refrigerator for 45–60 minutes before using.

VARIATION
Sweet Shortcrust Pastry: Omit salt and sift 4 tbsp caster sugar with flour.

Note that when a recipe in this book calls for a specific weight of pastry, the quantity refers to the total weight, not the amount of flour used.

1 Sift the flour and salt into a large mixing bowl. Cut the butter or margarine into even-sized pieces and add to the flour. To rub the fat into the flour, reach the fingertips down the sides of the bowl, bringing them together. As they meet lift the hands out of the

2 Add the water all at once, sprinkling it evenly over the surface, and stir together with the blade of a table knife until it forms large lumps.

3 Press together firmly with the fingers to form an even dough that leaves the sides of the bowl clean.

Rough Puff Pastry

Rough puff pastry is much more straightforward to make than puff pastry, and although it cannot compete with full puff pastry in making beautifully risen vol-au-vents, layered mille feuilles and fancy biscuits, rough puff is more than adequate for flaky pie coverings, turnovers, mince pies and sausage rolls.

Rough puff pastry is prepared in a similar way to shortcrust pastry. The main difference is that instead of rubbing the fat into the flour in small pieces, the cool butter or margarine is retained in hazelnut-sized pieces and incorporated into an even dough.

The flakiness of rough puff pastry is achieved by rolling the pastry out into a rectangle so as to flatten the pieces of firm fat into what amounts to a series of overlapping puddles, each interleaved with a layer of dough. As the pastry is folded neatly and rolled again and again, the layers of fat increase and the characteristic structure of the rough puff pastry is formed.

MAKES 450 g/1 lb
250 g/9 oz plain flour
1 generous pinch salt
175 g/6 oz cool butter or margarine
125 ml/4 fl oz cold water

1 Sift the flour and salt together into a large mixing bowl. Cut the butter or margarine into even pieces roughly the size of a hazelnut and toss lightly in the flour.

2 Add all of the water and stir into an even dough with a table

knife, taking care not to mutilate the pieces of fat. Turn the dough onto a floured surface and knead lightly. Wrap in cling film and rest in the refrigerator for 30 minutes.

3 Dust the pastry with flour and roll out into a long rectangle. Fold the pastry into three as if it were a business letter and turn it so that the two open ends are north and south. Dust with flour and repeat three times. Wrap the pastry in cling film and allow to rest in the refrigerator for 30 minutes before baking.

VARIATIONS
Rough puff pastry can be made with half wholemeal and half plain flour. If you wish to cut down on butter but retain some of the flavour, use half butter and half block margarine.

Rich Biscuit Pastry

Rich biscuit pastry has the advantage that it does not require lengthy resting times: it can be rolled out and baked as soon as it is made. Rich biscuit pastry has many applications although it is most widely used for sweet flans and tarts and coverings for fruit pies. The baked crust is less inclined to become soggy than shortcrust when in contact with moist fruit and soft fillings.

The secret of rich biscuit pastry is that, unlike shortcrust and rough puff pastry, no water is used in the recipe. The result is a short, non-elastic pastry that handles as easily as plasticine. The short nature of the pastry is determined by the high proportion of fat.

Rich biscuit pastry is best used when the fat is cool and plastic. If, however, the pastry is allowed to firm too much in the refrigerator, rolling may be difficult. If you find that the pastry is too hard to roll, simply beat it firmly with a rolling pin before use.

MAKES 350 g/12 oz
200 g/7 oz plain flour
125 g/4 oz cool unsalted butter or
　margarine
50 g/2 oz caster sugar
1 egg, size 3 or 4

1 Sift the flour into a large mixing bowl. Cut the firm butter or margarine into even-sized pieces and add to the flour followed by the caster sugar.

2 Rub the fat into the flour between the fingers until the mixture resembles large fresh breadcrumbs. (If you are using an electric food mixer or a food processor, take care not to over-do the rubbing in.)

3 Add the egg and combine into an even dough. Although it is not essential for rich biscuit pastry to rest, in warm weather it may be necessary to firm the pastry in the refrigerator for 20–30 minutes before using.

VARIATION
Failed rich biscuit pastry can be turned into the most delicious crumble topping. Simply add 100 g/4 oz of rolled oats to the disaster pastry and rub together evenly. Spread the topping over a combination of fresh fruit sweetened with sugar and bake in a moderate oven for 35–40 minutes.

WATCHPOINTS

ROLLING OUT PASTRY

1

Ensure that your rolling pin is straight and your work surface is flat before you begin.

2

Do not allow the pastry to stick to the work surface or it will not roll out evenly.

3

Small pieces of pastry are more manageable to roll out than ones that are very large.

4

Pastry will only roll into a circle if it starts off as a neat round.

5

Pastry that is rolled out too thinly is difficult to handle.

6

Never pick up pastry by the edges. Use the entire surface of a hand or a rolling pin.

7

Never leave rolled-out pastry for long in a warm kitchen.

BAKING

8

Always start baking in a hot oven; if necessary, the temperature can be lowered after a while to dry the pastry.

Rolling out pastry

1 Dust the work surface and pastry lightly but evenly with sifted flour. Shape your pastry into a

neat round, squash flat and roll out to a generous thickness, to the required shape.

2 As you are rolling ensure periodically that the pastry will move freely on the work surface. Work quickly and efficiently to retain the coolness of the pastry and use immediately.

Lining a Flan Tin

When lining a flan tin, the aim is to lay the pastry in the tin without stretching it. Metal flan rings are most convenient to use as they conduct heat particularly well, allow for a good depth of filling and can easily be removed after baking.

Loose-bottomed metal flan tins are also good. Glazed earthenware and porcelain dishes are poor conductors of heat and are often the cause of a soggy bottom. Allow a little extra baking time if you have to use one of these.

Allow 350 g/12 oz pastry to line a 20–23 cm/8–9 inch flan tin.

1 If using a flan ring, place it on a baking sheet. Roll out the pastry into a circle 10 cm/4 inches larger than the flan ring or tin.

2 To avoid stretching the pastry unnecessarily, lift the edges of the pastry towards the centre and push into the corners, turning the tin as you go. Press the pastry gently but firmly against the sides.

3 Firmly roll the rolling pin over the top of the tin to remove excess pastry from the edge.

4 To prevent the base of the pastry case from rising in the oven, prick it several times with a table fork. If using shortcrust or flaky

pastry, allow to rest in the refrigerator for 45–60 minutes before baking to prevent shrinking.

Baking Blind

Baking blind is the term used to describe baking a pastry case before filling it. To prevent the side of the pastry case from collapsing and the base from rising the pastry is covered with a circle of greaseproof paper and weighed down with dried beans or rice. Rich biscuit pastry is particularly suitable for baking blind because it dries more successfully than other pastries.

1 Cut a circle of greaseproof paper to fit in the pastry case and half fill with dried beans or rice. Bake in

the centre of a preheated 200°C/400°F/gas 6 oven for 15–20 minutes.

2 Lift out the paper together with the beans or rice. If the pastry base appears not to be dried out sufficiently, return the pastry case to

the bottom shelf of the oven to bake for a further 5–10 minutes.

Allow to cool on a wire rack. Store in an airtight container and use within 2–3 days.

Glazing

It is not absolutely essential to glaze pastry but it does improve its appearance when baked.

Beaten egg produces the most attractive glaze, although milk, or a mixture of milk and egg may be used. For an extra shiny glaze, add a

good pinch of salt to a beaten egg and stir until dissolved.

Brush the glaze lightly and evenly over the pastry, using a pastry brush. If you are applying pastry decorations, glaze these too.

Sweet shortcrust and flaky pastry may be glazed after baking by dusting with icing sugar and finishing under a hot grill.

Storing and Freezing Pastry

Pastry is best wrapped in cling film to be sure all air is excluded. It can be kept in the refrigerator for 2–3 days.

Uncooked pastry can be frozen successfully, and is best thawed and glazed before baking.

Apricot Custard Tart with Almonds

WATCHPOINTS

◆

Egg Custard ◆ Pastry

SERVES 6

1 recipe rich biscuit pastry (page 139)

50 g/2 oz ground almonds

900 g/2 lb apricots, halved and stoned

little caster sugar (optional)

Custard:

1 egg

1 tbsp caster sugar

2 drops almond essence

75 ml/3 fl oz single cream

When apricots are in season, try them baked in this delicious tart enriched with ground almonds and set with a smooth egg custard.

———— ◆ ————

Preheat the oven to 190°C/375°F/gas 5. Roll out the pastry on a floured work surface to a thickness of 6 mm/¼ inch and line a 23 cm/9 inch flan tin. Sprinkle the ground almonds over the pastry base and arrange the apricots, cut side down, on top. Bake in the preheated oven for 15–20 minutes.

Meanwhile, prepare the custard. Beat the egg with the sugar and almond essence and stir in the cream. Strain the custard over the apricots and bake for a further 10–15 minutes or until the custard has set. Serve warm or cold.

Bakewell Plum Tart

WATCHPOINTS

◆

Classic Sponge Cake ◆ Pastry

SERVES 6

1 recipe rich biscuit pastry (page 139)

225 g/8 oz dark plums

1 recipe frangipan sponge mixture (page 101)

In the town of Bakewell, in Derbyshire, you can still buy a Bakewell tart baked according to the original 19th-century recipe: a mixture of bread-crumbs, sugar, ground almonds and egg yolks spread over a layer of red jam in a pastry shell. I hope the inhabitants of Bakewell will forgive my version — a layer of plums covered with a rich almond frangipan decorated with strips of leftover pastry. Not quite the original but delicious all the same.

———— ◆ ————

Roll out the pastry on a lightly floured surface to a thickness of 3 mm/⅛ inch and use to line a 23 cm/9 inch metal flan tin, without stretching the pastry. Trim off the excess pastry and reserve.

Preheat the oven to 190°C/375°F/gas 5. Cut the plums in half and remove the stones. Scatter the plums over the bottom of the flan case. Cover with the frangipan and smooth evenly. Decorate with pastry strips cut from the trimmings. Bake in the preheated oven for 40–45 minutes or until a skewer inserted into the centre will come away cleanly. Serve warm or cold with vanilla ice cream or custard.

Bakewell Plum Tart;
Apricot Custard Tart
with Almonds.

Fresh Peaches in a Frangipane Flan

SERVES 6

1 recipe sweet shortcrust pastry
    (page 137)

Frangipane filling:

275 ml/¹/₂ pint milk

¹/₂ vanilla pod, split open, or 2–3
    drops vanilla essence

3 egg yolks

2 tbsp caster sugar

4 tbsp plain flour

8 small macaroons, crushed

Topping:

6 ripe peaches, skinned

4 tbsp apricot jam, to glaze

A wonderful concoction – fresh peaches baked on a layer of frangipane cream – delicious vanilla-scented custard, riddled with crushed macaroons.

———— ◆ ————

Roll out the pastry on a lightly floured work surface to a thickness of 3 mm/¹/₈ inch and use to line a 23 cm/9 inch flan tin. Rest in the refrigerator for 45 minutes.

To make the filling, put 2 tbsp of the milk in a bowl. Put the remainder of the milk in a heavy saucepan, add the vanilla pod or essence and bring to the boil. Add the egg yolks, sugar and flour to the milk in the bowl and stir until smooth. When the milk has come to the boil, pour it over the egg mixture, stirring. Return to the saucepan and simmer, stirring, for 3–4 minutes to thicken. Stir in the crushed macaroons, cover and set aside.

Preheat the oven to 190°C/375°F/gas 5. Line the flan case with greaseproof paper, fill with baking beans and bake blind for 25 minutes.

Spread the frangipane cream in the flan case, cover with the peach halves and bake for 35 minutes. To glaze, heat the apricot jam until melted and brush over the peaches. Serve warm or cold with a raspberry purée.

Fresh Peaches in a Frangipane Flan; Almond and Mincemeat Tart.

Almond and Mincemeat Tart

SERVES 6

1 recipe sweet shortcrust pastry
    (page 137)

200 g/7 oz mincemeat

1 recipe frangipan sponge mixture
    (page 101)

50 g/2 oz flaked almonds

icing sugar for dusting

A quick, easy and delicious way to use up leftover mincemeat after Christmas is to spread it in a pastry case, cover with a layer of frangipan sponge and bake to perfection. The result is beautifully moist and spicy.

———— ◆ ————

Roll out the pastry on a lightly floured work surface to a thickness of 3 mm/¹/₈ inch and use to line a 23 cm/9 inch metal flan tin. Rest in the refrigerator for at least 45 minutes.

Preheat the oven to 190°C/375°F/gas 5. Spread the mincemeat over the bottom of the flan case. Cover with the frangipan and scatter over the almonds. Bake in the preheated oven for 35–40 minutes, or until a skewer inserted in the centre comes away cleanly. Dust with icing sugar to serve.

Lemon Chiffon Pie with Berry Fruits

WATCHPOINTS

Pastry ◆ Meringue ◆ Egg Custard

SERVES 6

1 recipe rich biscuit pastry (page 139), or sweet shortcrust pastry (page 137)

2 tbsp strawberry or raspberry jam

200 ml/7 fl oz milk

3 eggs, at room temperature, separated

75 g/3 oz caster sugar

1 tbsp plain flour

finely grated zest and juice of 2 small lemons

2 tsp powdered gelatine

2 tbsp cold water

225 g/8 oz ripe berry fruits, such as strawberries, raspberries, blackcurrants, redcurrants, blackberries

To decorate:

ripe berry fruits, such as redcurrants, raspberries or strawberries

Lemon desserts are very popular for dinner parties providing, of course, they are not too sweet. For this old favourite I have replaced some of the sugar with seasonal berry fruits, which add both colour and flavour to this already delicious dessert.

————————— ◆ —————————

Preheat the oven to 200°C/400°F/gas 6. Roll out the pastry and use to line a 20 cm/8 inch loose-based flan tin. Line with a circle of greaseproof paper and dried beans, then bake blind for 20–30 minutes. Allow the flan case to cool completely.

Spread the jam evenly over the bottom of the pastry case with the back of a spoon and set aside.

Measure 2 tbsp of the milk into a mixing bowl. Pour the remainder into a heavy saucepan and bring to the boil. Add the egg yolks, 50 g/2 oz of the caster sugar and the flour to the milk in the mixing bowl. Add the lemon zest and juice and stir with a hand whisk until smooth. Pour the hot milk over the mixture and stir until even. Return to the saucepan and bring back to the boil, stirring constantly. Simmer for 1–2 minutes, stirring. Remove from the heat.

Sprinkle the powdered gelatine into a small cup containing the cold water, leave for a few minutes to soften, then stir into the hot lemon mixture until dissolved.

Whisk the egg whites in a clean bowl until they will hold their weight on the whisk. Add the remaining sugar a little at a time and continue whisking until stiff. Fold the egg whites into the warm lemon mixture using a large metal spoon or spatula. Fold in the berry fruits.

Turn into the flan case over the layer of jam, and spread out evenly. Allow to cool, then chill until the filling has set. Before serving, decorate the top with extra fruits.

Illustrated on page 134

Note: When berry fruits are out of season, use frozen ones or stoned bottled cherries instead.

Lindy's Skyscraper Cheesecake

SERVES 10–12

1 recipe rich biscuit pastry (page 139)

Filling:

700 g/1¹⁄₂ lb full fat soft cheese

225 ml/8 fl oz soured cream

150 g/5 oz caster sugar

1 tbsp plain flour

3 whole eggs

2 egg yolks

finely grated zest and juice of 1 orange

finely grated zest and juice of 1 lemon

1 tsp vanilla essence

To decorate:

strawberries

Hidden away in the heart of New York City is a family-run restaurant and coffee shop that has a well-earned reputation for an awe-inspiring cheesecake. Each slice stands as tall and as impressive as the glass-fronted buildings that ascend dizzily from the busy sidewalks of this city. While the original recipe for Lindy's cheesecake remains a closely guarded secret, there have been many attempts to recreate it elsewhere. Here is my version.

———————— ◆ ————————

Roll out a little over half of the pastry and use to line the bottom of a 20 cm/8 inch loose-bottomed cake tin. Shape the remainder of the pastry into a sausage, roll into a long strip and use to line the side of the tin. This is best done by cutting the strip of pastry into manageable lengths and overlapping piece by piece against the side of the tin. Place the lined tin in the refrigerator to rest the pastry while you make the filling. Preheat the oven to 220°C/425°F/gas 7.

Blend the soft cheese together with the soured cream, sugar, flour, eggs and egg yolks until smooth. Add the orange and lemon zest followed by the citrus juices and vanilla essence.

Turn the filling into the pastry-lined tin and bake in the preheated oven for 15 minutes. Lower the temperature to 140°C/275°F/gas 1 and bake for a further 1¹⁄₂–1³⁄₄ hours. The initial high temperature is necessary to ensure that the mixture rises sufficiently to gain lightness. Leave to cool completely in the tin.

To serve, carefully remove the cheesecake from the tin and transfer to a serving plate. Decorate the edge with a border of sliced strawberries. The cheesecake will keep for several days in a cool place; it does not freeze well.

Illustrated on page 134

Note: As this cheesecake cools it will shrink away slightly from the edges of the pastry case. The decorative strawberry border conveniently conceals the gap. The pastry case is very delicate, so take care when removing the cheesecake from the tin.

Ice Cream Profiteroles
with Hot Chocolate Sauce

WATCHPOINTS
◆
Choux Pastry

SERVES 6

soft butter for greasing

1 recipe choux pastry (page 149)

1 quantity vanilla ice cream (page 53)

Chocolate sauce:

150 ml/5 fl oz single cream or milk

1 tbsp caster sugar

175 g/6 oz best quality plain chocolate, chopped

Piping hot chocolate sauce poured slowly over a pile of profiteroles filled with vanilla ice cream, is the perfect finale to a successful meal.

————— ◆ —————

Preheat the oven to 200°C/400°F/gas 6. Lightly grease two large baking sheets.

Spoon or pipe the choux pastry batter into little heaps no bigger than a walnut in its shell, onto the baking sheets, spacing two finger widths apart. Bake one sheet at a time in the centre of the preheated oven for 25–30 minutes. Allow to cool on a wire rack.

Split each profiterole open and fill with vanilla ice cream. Place in the freezer until ready to serve.

To prepare the hot chocolate sauce, put the cream and caster sugar in a small saucepan and bring to the boil. Remove the pan from the heat, add the chocolate and stir until melted.

To serve, pile the profiteroles in a serving dish and pour over the hot chocolate sauce. Serve immediately

Chocolate Éclairs

WATCHPOINTS
◆
Choux Pastry ◆ Crème Pâtissière

MAKES 12

soft butter for greasing

1 recipe choux pastry (page 149)

1 recipe crème diplomat (page 27) or 275 ml/10 fl oz whipping cream, whipped

Chocolate topping:

4 tbsp caster sugar

3 tbsp water

175 g/6 oz best quality plain chocolate, chopped

Those of us who were not dreaming of cream cakes during French lessons at school will know that *un 'éclair* is a flash of lightning. Small boys must stop and wonder as they gaze into cake shop windows whether the word éclair is used to describe the speed at which these pastry fingers are baked or whether it has to do with the rate at which they may be eaten.

————— ◆ —————

Preheat the oven to 200°C/400°F/gas 6. Lightly grease two baking sheets and set aside.

Put the choux pastry into a piping bag fitted with a 2 cm/³/₄ inch plain nozzle.

Ice Cream Profiteroles with Hot Chocolate Sauce

Hold the piping bag as near parallel to the baking sheet as possible, resting the nozzle on your thumb. Pipe a length of about 10 cm/4 inches, as round as possible. Cut the end of the éclair by placing your index finger over the end of the nozzle. Pipe the éclairs six to a baking sheet, and bake one sheet at a time in the preheated oven for 30–40 minutes. Allow to cool on a wire rack.

To prepare the chocolate topping, measure the caster sugar and water into a small saucepan and bring to a simmer. Remove from the heat and stir in the chocolate until melted.

To fill the éclairs, split them open down one side and spoon or pipe the crème diplomat or whipped cream into each. Dip the top of the éclairs into the chocolate to coat and leave to set before serving.

Illustrated on page 153

Gâteau Paris-Brest

WATCHPOINTS

◆

Choux Pastry ◆ Crème Pâtissière

SERVES 6
soft butter for greasing
1 recipe choux pastry (page 149)
1 egg
1 pinch salt
25 g/1 oz flaked almonds
1 recipe almond crème pâtissière
    (page 27)
icing sugar for dusting

Once a year, the French stage a bicycle race from Paris to Brest, stretching some 600 km across the bumpy roads of Normandy and Brittany. True to form, an unknown pastry-cook at the turn of the century saw fit to create a circular cake in the shape of a bicycle wheel. A ring of choux pastry was sprinkled with chopped almonds, baked, split open and filled with a flavoured pastry cream. While legendary pastry-cooks rest in heaven, their creations live to see another day.

——— ◆ ———

Preheat the oven to 200°C/400°F/gas 6. Lightly grease a baking sheet with soft butter. Lightly grease a 23 cm/9 inch flan ring, place it on the baking sheet and set aside. (If you prefer to pipe or spoon the choux pastry free-hand, you won't need the flan ring.)

Spoon the choux pastry batter into a piping bag fitted with a 2 cm/³⁄₄ inch plain nozzle and pipe a single ring inside the flan ring. Pipe a second ring inside, adjacent to the first, then pipe a third on top. Beat the egg with the salt and brush over the pastry evenly. Sprinkle with the flaked almonds.

Bake in the centre of the preheated oven for 45–50 minutes. Make sure that the ring is sufficiently dry before taking it out of the oven. If in doubt, lower the temperature to 180°C/350°F/gas 4 and bake for a further 10–15 minutes. Allow to cool on a wire rack.

Slice the ring horizontally in half and remove any uncooked choux dough from inside. Sandwich back together with almond crème pâtissière. Dust with sifted icing sugar and serve.

Note that the unfilled choux pastry ring will keep in an airtight container for up to 3 days or it may be frozen until required. Crisp in a preheated hot oven at 200°C/400°F/gas 6 for 8–10 minutes before using.

Illustrated on page 135

VARIATION
Try Paris-Brest filled with crème diplomat, chocolate or praline crème pâtissière or sweetened whipped cream.

Dessert Biscuits

Crisp, light dessert biscuits are the perfect accompaniments to ices, sorbets and fresh fruit desserts. I have therefore included a few of my favourite ones to complement appropriate desserts. Both almond tuiles and brandy snaps can be set in basket shapes and filled with ice creams, sorbets and fruit confections.

Almond Tuiles

MAKES 24

50 g/2 oz butter, plus extra for greasing
125 g/4 oz icing sugar
2 egg whites
½ tsp almond essence
50 g/2 oz plain flour
50 g/2 oz flaked almonds, toasted

This biscuit takes its name from its resemblance to the curved roof tiles (*tuiles*) of the south of France. Almond tuiles are popular not only because they are deliciously light and crisp, but because they are both quick and easy to make. Traditionally, almond tuiles are served with ice creams and sorbets, although they may also be served as a petit four.

——————— ◆ ———————

Preheat the oven to 200°C/400°F/gas 6. Lightly grease two heavy baking sheets with butter and set aside.

Measure the butter into a mixing bowl set over a saucepan of boiling water and half melt, for no longer than 1 minute. Remove the bowl from the hot water and stir until the butter is the consistency of loosely whipped cream. Sift in the icing sugar and combine evenly. Add the egg whites one at a time, stirring until even. Add the almond essence, and stir in the flour to form a smooth batter.

Spoon the mixture into little heaps on the prepared baking sheets, six to each baking sheet. Sprinkle with flaked almonds. Bake, one sheet at a time, near the top of the oven for 5 minutes or until the biscuits are golden brown around the edges. Without delay, remove the biscuits from the baking sheet using a palette knife and set on the curved shape of a rolling pin.

When cool and set, carefully lift off the tuiles and store in an airtight container until ready to serve.

VARIATION
By spooning the mixture into larger heaps, the resulting bigger tuiles may be formed into basket shapes. Bake no more than three to a sheet. As soon as they are cooked, remove the tuiles from the baking sheet and mould each one over the base of an upturned glass. Leave until set.

Tuile baskets may be used to serve ice creams and sorbets.

Langues de Chat

MAKES 48

50 g/2 oz butter, plus extra for
  greasing
$^1/_2$ vanilla pod, or $^1/_2$ tsp vanilla
  essence
50 g/2 oz caster sugar
2 egg whites, at room temperature
50 g/2 oz plain flour

Langues de chat, or 'cat's tongues', are very popular served with ice creams and sorbets. They are at their best served straight from the oven, although they will keep for up to 2 weeks in an airtight container.

———————— ◆ ————————

Preheat the oven to 200°C/400°F/gas 6. Lightly grease two baking sheets with butter. Soften the butter and beat until it is the consistency of loosely whipped cream. Set aside.

Split the vanilla pod open and scrape out the black paste on to a wooden board. Add 1 tsp of the caster sugar and rub the paste evenly into the sugar with the side of a small knife. Add this, or the vanilla essence if using, together with the remaining sugar to the soft butter. Beat together with a wooden spoon until the mixture is light, 2–3 minutes. Add the egg whites a little at a time, beating well. Add the flour and mix to a smooth batter.

Spoon the mixture into a piping bag fitted with a 6 mm/$^1/_4$ inch plain nozzle. Pipe into 7.5 cm/3 inch lengths on the prepared baking sheets, keeping each length a finger's width apart. Bake on the top shelf of the pre-heated oven for 6–8 minutes or until golden brown at the edges. Transfer the biscuits to a wire rack whilst they are still warm and allow to cool.

Brandy Snaps

MAKES 36

50 g/2 oz butter, plus extra for
  greasing
125 g/4 oz caster sugar
50 g/2 oz golden syrup
50 g/2 oz plain flour
$^1/_2$ tsp ground ginger

Brandy snaps can be set into a variety of attractive shapes. Try setting them in individual tartlet tins to form baskets.

———————— ◆ ————————

Preheat the oven to 200°C/400°F/gas 6. Lightly grease two heavy baking sheets with butter.

Place the butter in a bowl over a pan of boiling water and half melt, no longer than 1 minute. Stir off the heat until the butter is the consistency of loosely whipped cream, then stir in the sugar and golden syrup. Sift the flour and ginger together and stir into the mixture to make a stiff paste.

Divide the paste into pieces no bigger than a grape, and bake three to a baking sheet in the preheated oven for 8–10 minutes or until golden brown and bubbly. Allow to cool on the baking sheets for a few seconds until beginning to set, then turn the biscuits over with a palette knife and roll each around the handle of a wooden spoon. Cool on a wire rack.

INDEX

———— ◆ ————